The Little Book
of

HANDY

HINTS

The Little Book
of

HANDY
HINTS

Edited by
ESTHER SELSDON

Special Edition for PAST TIMES®, 2000

Published by Parragon

Parragon
Queen Street House
4 Queen Street
Bath BA1 1HE, UK

Produced by Magpie Books, an imprint of
Constable & Robinson Ltd, London

Copyright © Parragon 2000

Cover illustration courtesy of Superstock

ISBN 0-75254-085-8

A copy of the British Library Cataloguing-in-Publication Data
is available from the British Library

Printed in China

PAST TIMES®

Contents

Introduction

A rule of thumb is a pithy epithet containing a general guideline to life based on experience rather than science. We all need and use such handy hints on a daily basis. They may not be strictly accurate and they may not be totally serious but they do enable the recipient to make an educated guess at what to do, say or expect next in any given situation. They may be silly or even obscure but, like all good folklore, they are based on a real event that a friend of someone you know experienced somewhere near you. They may be trivial but they are entertaining and they may even be useful.

Chapter 1

ABOUT THE SELF

Life would be infinitely easier if we could only be born aged eighty and gradually approach eighteen.

Mark Twain

Aging
Bodies age, emotions don't.

Beards
The only time you'll ever know what people really think of your beard is after you've shaved it off.

Behavior
If the only tool you have is a hammer, you treat everything in life like a nail.

Belief
Men prefer to believe what they prefer to be true.

Big bums

Texture and sheen make your bum look bigger; smooth and dull make you look smaller. This is why most of us should never wear skintight, pink satin trousers.

Blushing

Man is the only creature that blushes.

Body heat

Sixty per cent of your body heat is lost through your head.

Brushing hair
Twenty-five brush strokes per day is considered optimal for the best distribution of natural oils. Any less will cause tangled hair, any more will cause damage.

Brushing your teeth
You will always run out of toothpaste on the morning of an appointment with the dentist.

Calories I
Carbohydrates and protein foods contain about one hundred calories per ounce. Fatty foods contain about two hundred calories per ounce.

Calories II
The average person resting comfortably for twenty-four hours will burn up about 1,700 calories.

Catching a cold
You will always catch a cold within two weeks of starting a new job.

Change
Any change seems terrible at first.

Checking a beer belly
Measure the circumference of your waist and hips. If your waist-to-hips ratio is over 1.0 (for men) or above 0.8 (for women), your risk of heart attack or stroke is five to ten times greater than if the ratio is lower.

Chest pain

If applying pressure with your fingers causes a change in chest pain, it is probably muscular.

Checking your ear lobes

If your ear lobes have a diagonal crease, you may have clogged coronary arteries.

Checking your pockets

It takes almost twice as long to find something in your coat pockets when you are not wearing your coat than when you are wearing it. If your coat has more than four pockets, you can usually save time by putting it on just to look through the pockets.

Decisions

If you are unable to decide between two alternatives, choose the cheaper one.

Dieting

Most overeating happens in the evening. If you can't diet all day, diet after dark.

Doctors
Just because your doctor has a name for your condition does not mean that he knows what it is.

Driving
The harder it is to stay awake on the drive home, the harder it will be to fall asleep when you get there.

Eating
Most people eat their biggest meal of the day at dinner time when their bodies need it least. Eat breakfast like a king, lunch like a prince and dinner like a pauper.

Experience

Whatever happens to you, it will previously have happened to everyone you know – only more so.

Families

The first half of our life is ruined by our parents and the second half by our children.

Feeling your age

You are middle-aged when your school days are featured as nostalgia on television. You are old when your wedding presents classify as antiques.

Final decisions

All our final decisions are made in a state of mind that is not going to last.

Fingernails

The longer your fingers, the faster your nails grow.

Foot size

The distance from your elbow to your wrist equals the length of your foot.

Foreign affairs

Nothing stimulates an interest in foreign affairs quite so intensely as having a son of military service age.

Gall bladders

White women with blonde hair, light skin and pale eyes are the most likely victims of gall bladder problems.

Genius

In every work of genius we recognize our rejected thoughts.

Getting dressed

Wearing dark colors below the waist and light colors above is usually more visually appealing than the other way around.

Getting lost
If you don't care where you are, then you aren't lost.

Giving your age
Odd-numbered ages seem older and wiser than even-numbered ages.

Glory
Glory may be fleeting but obscurity is forever.

Hair loss
Normal daily hair loss is one hundred to two hundred hairs per day.

Happiness I
Happiness is not a goal; it is a by-product.

Happiness II
Genuine ecstasy occurs on discovering that you haven't lost your wallet after all.

Having a go
Nothing will ever be attempted if all possible objections must first be overcome.

Heart beats

Always take a note of your heartbeat at rest first thing in the morning. An increase of seven beats per minute is a sign of overtraining.

Heart rates

Your maximum safe heart rate is equal to 220 minus your age. For example, a forty-year-old should have a maximum heart rate of 220-40 = 180 beats per minute. Your target heart rate for aerobic exercise is equal to 160 minus your age.

Height

The distance between your fingertips, with your arms outstretched at shoulder height, is equal to your height.

Hospitals

For every day you spend in the hospital, you need one week to recuperate.

Inertia

Inertia has its own momentum.

Information

The degree to which you overreact to information will be in inverse proportion to its accuracy.

Intuition

Intuition is reason in a hurry.

Irritation
Nothing is more irritating than not being invited to a party you wouldn't be seen dead at.

Jogging
If you can run one and a half miles in twelve minutes, six days a week, you can run any distance you like.

Income
The cost of living will always rise to exceed your income.

Injuries

For pulled muscles, twisted joints and other musculoskeletal injuries, use ice on new injuries, heat on old ones.

Investment I

A fool and your money are soon partners.

Investment II

You may know where the market is going today but you can't know where it's going after that.

Labor I
The more elaborate and efficient the arrangements you have made to have your baby at home, the more likely your waters are to break in a supermarket.

Labor II
Labor has the euphoria of a first night. Parenthood runs as long as a hit musical with no cast changes.

Lifts
Whichever way you turn on entering a lift, the buttons will be on the opposite side.

Listening
If people listened to themselves more often, they would talk less.

Lists

Make a new "do it today" list every day for ten days. If an item gets transferred from one list to the next and is still on the list at the end of the ten days, then drop it.

Loneliness

When you are lonely, make a horrible mess of your home and desirable company is sure to arrive immediately.

Mae West's dictum
To err is human but it feels divine.

Man
Man is an animal that makes bargains; no other animal does this – no dog exchanges bones with another.

Medical tests
Before asking for a medical test ask yourself what you will do if the result is either positive or negative. If both answers are identical then don't bother with the test.

Motherhood
Any mother with only two arms is handicapped.

Muscle and fat
About 40 per cent of your body weight is muscle. If you swap 9 pounds of muscle for 9 pounds of fat, you will shrink by about 1 per cent because muscle is denser.

Music
In real life there is no background music.

Need
You get the most of what you need the least.

Newspapers
If you don't read a newspaper on the day you bought it, bin it. You'll never go back and read it again.

Panic
If you can keep your head when all about you are losing theirs, then you probably haven't understood the problem.

Personal finances
If you're wondering whether you have enough money to take the family out to a restaurant this evening, then you haven't.

Pessimism
There is a fine line between pessimism and realism.

Plans I
No plan is fixed in stone.

Plans II
Never change your plans because of the weather.

Pregnancy
Book the trip of a lifetime. You will be pregnant before the tickets arrive.

Probability
The probability of anything happening is in inverse ratio to its desirability.

Punctuality
Punctuality is the virtue of the bored.

Purchasing power
The purchase of any product can be justified if the desire to own it is intense enough.

Questions

Asking stupid questions is easier than correcting stupid mistakes.

Queuing

If you switch queues, the one you just left will start to move faster than the one you are now in.

Reflection

He who hesitates is probably right.

Selecting clothes

If you can't decide between two alternatives — a blue suit and a gray one, for example, toss a coin. If the coin comes down and you have the least inclination to make it two out of three tosses, you know it's the other suit that you really want to wear.

Sex changes

A man who changes his sex will look like a woman who is five years older because men's faces look more rugged than women's. A female who changes her sex to a male, however, will look like a man ten to twelve years younger.

Shaving

Your face is dry and puffy when you first wake up in the morning. Delay shaving for two minutes for every hour that you were asleep.

Silence

It is better to keep your mouth shut and to appear stupid than to open it and remove all doubt.

Silly games

When a man says it's a silly game, it's probably something at which his wife can beat him.

Simplicity

The simplest subjects are the ones you don't know anything about.

Sincerity

The secret of success is sincerity. Once you can fake that you've got it made.

Sleep

Whatever time you go to bed, you will never feel like you've had quite enough sleep.

Success I

The penalty of success is to be bored by the people who used to snub you.

Success II

If at first you do succeed, try to hide your astonishment.

Survival

You can live three seconds without blood, three minutes without air, three days without water and three weeks without food.

Taking action

Find two good reasons for following a course of action; you can always find one.

Telephones

The telephone will always ring the second you get into the bath.

Virtue

Virtue is its own punishment.

Waiting for a doctor

To be safe, plan on sitting around for at least an hour on any visit to a doctor or dentist. You can save yourself time by taking the first appointment of the day or the first appointment after lunch.

Waiting rooms – general

The more boring and out-of-date the magazines in a waiting room, the longer you will have to wait for your scheduled appointment.

Winning the lottery

The person who takes comfort in the overwhelming odds against being hit by lightning will be convinced the same odds cannot prevent him from winning the lottery.

Wisdom

Wisdom consists of knowing when to avoid perfection.

Worrying

Don't worry about what other people are thinking about you. They're too busy worrying about what you think about them.

Chapter 2

ABOUT OTHERS

Nothing needs so reforming as other people's habits.

Mark Twain

Ability
Those who can, do. Those who can't, teach.

Accepting an engagement ring
The cost of an engagement ring was once considered to be crucial to a gentleman's intentions. A suitor was expected to spend one month's wages on a ring. A young man who spent less than this was probably a scoundrel; one who spent more was a show-off.

Accepting invitations
Accept all invitations, even to occasions in which you have no interest, because half of all social arrangements fall through and you will get credit for being friendly. You never know what might come out of the half that do not.

Addressing the clergy
Always call a Roman Catholic priest "Father" unless he is wearing some purple. Then call him "Bishop" or "your excellency."

Ambition
A woman who strives to be like a man lacks ambition.

Anger
Never try to pacify someone at the height of their rage.

Answering calls
Usually a telephone caller makes three points. The third one is the real reason for the call.

Archaeologists

An archaeologist is the best husband a woman can have. The older she is, the more interested in her he will be.

Arranging a date

Always get the other person's phone number – just in case you want to call it off.

Arrogance

Arrogance is too often the companion of excellence.

Asking permission

It is generally easier to ask for forgiveness than for permission.

Avoiding lunatics

To avoid lunatics on city buses, sit in the middle of the bus. The friendly lunatics sit as close to the driver as they can, the unfriendly ones sit as far away as possible.

Babies
When your baby eventually falls asleep in your lap and suddenly looks charming for the first time in two hours, the telephone will immediately ring on the other side of the room.

Baby digestion
Much of what goes in must, eventually, come out but not necessarily by the expected route.

Behavior
If someone says "it's not the money, it's the principle" then it's really the money.

Birthdays

The richer the relative, the easier it is to remember their birthday.

Blind dates

If a blind date describes themselves as "sweet, friendly and intelligent," their physical appearance will, generally, not be their best feature.

Borrowing

Never lend a possession unless you borrow an item of equal importance at the same time.

Boys

The biggest difference between men and boys is the cost of their toys.

Bumping into people
The probability of meeting someone you know increases when you are with someone with whom you do not wish to be seen.

Checking sincerity
Genuine emotion is always expressed with the entire body. When uncertain of a person's motivations, watch their shoulders. You should not trust anyone who is speaking passionately but has relaxed shoulders.

Children I
A child will become as you describe him to others.

Children II

One child is not enough but two children is far too many.

Children III

Just because they don't know the word for it, doesn't mean they can't do it.

Choosing pets

The age of a child is inversely correlated with the size of the animals it prefers.

Choosing – sex of child
For a girl eat endless dairy products and drink no coffee. For a boy eat vegetables and drink no citrus juice.

Cinemas
At any screening, the people whose seats are furthest from the aisle will always arrive last.

Collecting children from parties
Every ten minutes that you delay going to pick up your children from a friend's party erodes your friendship with their parents by one year.

Conservatives

A conservative is someone who admires radicals a century after they're dead.

Conversation I

If you don't want your children to hear what you are saying, pretend you're talking to them.

Conversation II

Two monologues do not make a dialogue.

Convincing others

If you cannot convince them, confuse them.

Corruption I
The amount of corruption in a society is directly proportional to the number of laws that the society has.

Corruption II
Government corruption is always reported in the past tense.

Creative people
A creative person is thirty-five times more likely than the average person to need treatment for a mental problem.

Daughters

It is a great mystery of life that the nincompoop that your daughter married is also the father of the most intelligent grandchildren in the country.

Decor

It is possible to tell the age of the children of a house by the height of the breakable objects from the floor.

Development

Up to the age of three, girls attain each development milestone three months earlier than boys.

Divorce

Divorce is an act of liberation. For the man, freedom to pursue his girlfriend, career and record collection. For the woman, freedom to clear up after the children, the pets and the burst washing machine.

Driving

Eighty per cent of all people consider themselves to be above average drivers.

Enemies I

Friends come and go but enemies accumulate.

Enemies II
It's far easier to forgive an enemy after you've got even with him.

Ethnic food
The ingredients of an authentic peasant dish will cripple any budget outside its country of origin.

Eyelashes
The youngest child has the longest eyelashes.

Families

Families who choose to have babies and families who choose not to have babies always feel sorry for each other.

Farmer's credo

Sow your wild oats on a Saturday night. On a Sunday pray for crop failure.

Fathers

The man who marries to have children divorces his wife for giving them too much attention.

First date
The spot never appears until an hour before the first date.

Flattery
When flattering women, it pays to be subtle. Men believe any compliment automatically.

Fools
A fool and his money are invited everywhere.

Friends I
You can still consider someone your friend if you know their home phone number by heart.

Friends II
Friends are people who know all about you and still like you.

Friends in need
If you help a friend in need, she is sure to remember you – the next time she's in need.

Getting emotionally involved
If you need to talk about it, you probably shouldn't do it.

Getting engaged

If your fiancé does something that annoys you before you're married, it will annoy you ten times more afterwards.

Getting things done

One has to resign oneself to being a nuisance if one wants to get anything done.

Gossip

Gossip is hearing something you like about someone you don't.

Grandchildren
Grandchildren grow up more quickly than children.

Guests
Your least wanted guests always leave last.

Heredity
The law of heredity is that all undesirable traits come from the other parent.

Housewives
Every housewife has her blind spot. This will prove to be her mother-in-law's bugbear.

Husbands

Husbands are like fires. They go out when unattended.

Information

Whenever you tell someone what you paid for any given item, you will always immediately find out where you could have bought the same thing for less money.

Inheritance

Where there's a will, there are relations.

In-laws
You will never be able to drink enough of your in-laws' alcohol to get even.

Jehovah's Witnesses
If there is only just enough time to complete a task, the Jehovah's Witnesses will call.

Jokes
He who laughs loudest probably didn't get the joke.

Keeping up

Don't try to keep up with the Joneses. Drag them down, it's cheaper.

Lending books

Never lend a book to a friend expecting ever to get it back.

Losing an argument

The first person to raise his voice will invariably lose the argument.

Making friends with a dog
If you want to be friends with somebody else's dog, let the dog make the first move and don't be too quick to respond.

Malice
Never attribute to malice what could adequately be explained by stupidity.

Marriage
Loose change on the kitchen table is communal property.

Memory

You will remember only 10 per cent of what you think you learned in college.

~ ❦ ~

Men in bars

If he's charming, sophisticated, handsome and well-dressed, he's almost certainly gay.

~ ❦ ~

Moral indignation

Moral indignation is jealousy with a halo.

~ ❦ ~

More behavior

The best predictor of future behavior is past behavior.

Mother love

Mother love reaches its peak when awaiting the return of a child from school, college or a holiday in a foreign country. It returns to normal levels about five minutes later.

Mothers

You can fool some of the people all of the time and all of the people some of the time but you can't fool your mother.

Mothers-in-law I

At least 50 per cent of the human race does not want their mother-in-law within walking distance.

Mothers-in-law II

Behind every successful man stands a surprised mother-in-law.

Names

All parents will call their children arbitrarily by whichever of their children's names springs to mind first.

Negative questions

If you ask a negative question, you will get a negative answer.

Negotiation
Say no, then negotiate.

New babies I
If they're happy, leave them alone.

New babies II
If they're crying, feed them.

New babies III
If they're asleep, take a nap.

New jobs
When starting a new job, beware of those who are too friendly, too soon.

Noisy cars
There is an inverse relationship between the intelligence of the driver and the noise made by that driver's vehicle.

Offending people
The people who offend others most easily are often the most easily offended themselves.

Offering advice I
Most people don't really want advice. If someone responds to three valid suggestions with a "yes, but . . ." then he or she is more interested in playing games than solving problems.

Offering advice II
The closer the relative, the more unwanted the advice.

Old maids
Being an old maid is like death by drowning – a really delightful sensation after you cease to struggle.

Parenting

If you want your children to turn out well, spend twice as much time with them as you think you should and half the amount of money.

Parents I

By the time you're right, you're dead.

Parents II

It is easier to love one's parents by letter.

Parents' friends
The children of your parents' friends are always
nerds.

Partners
Most partners deserve each other.

Passion
A grand passion rarely survives a stuck zipper.

People
When people are free to do as they please, they
usually imitate each other.

Philanderers

Men who leave home for another woman are always astonished when their wives don't want them back.

Possibilities

Nothing is impossible for the man who doesn't have to do it himself.

Presents

People who give your child cymbals, electronic games or water pistols have no children themselves.

Prospective partners I
Never ring a prospective partner on a Friday, a Saturday or before 5 p.m. on a Sunday. Tuesday or Wednesday evenings are optimum.

Prospective partners II
Always wait at least two days before replying to a prospective partner's answering machine message. And always sound surprised when this time lapse is pointed out to you.

Quiet children
Even quiet children turn into teenagers.

Relatives
We all like our relatives when we're under five.

Repetition
Repetition does not establish validity.

Reunions
The person who has to travel furthest always arrives first.

Romantic gestures
Other people's romantic gestures seem exciting. Your own always come out clumsy and awkward.

Sausages
People who love sausages and respect the law should never watch either being made.

Saying things
People will lapse into silence after every twenty minutes of conversation.

Saying other things

If you find yourself thinking that something goes without saying, it is probably in the best interests of everyone involved to say it.

Schools

Girls do better at single-sex schools. Boys do better at mixed-sex schools.

Self-defense

When you are being attacked by several assailants at the same time, respond to the largest one first by sticking your fingers in one or both of his or her eyes. This will frighten the others enough to give you time to run away.

Self-help groups
Do not join self-help groups. If you enjoy feeling inadequate then call your mother.

Sex
Put one pebble in a jar for every time you have sex in the first year of marriage. Take one pebble out every time you have sex thereafter. You'll never empty that jar.

Sex – of children
Couples with two children of the same sex will generally have a third child also of the same sex.

Shy children

Any shy child will choose an incredibly crowded, extremely public arena to demonstrate its newly acquired rude words (at great volume).

Siblings

Where there's a sibling, there's quibbling.

Sick children

A parent who sends a child to school on the understanding that the child should call if he or she is not feeling better soon should always expect that call.

Sleep

Never put your head around the baby's door to check if she is asleep. She was.

Snoring

The spouse who snores loudest always falls asleep first.

Social situations

In an awkward social situation that which is most difficult to do is usually the right thing to do.

Solitude

Nobody will leave you alone – until you need a friend.

Staring

Two people who stare each other in the eye for sixty seconds without flinching will soon either fall out or start dating.

Strokes

You are most likely to suffer a stroke or a heart attack between eight and nine in the morning.

Systems
New systems generate new problems.

Talking to foreigners
When talking to people who do not speak your own native language fluently, always assume that they understand about half as much as they look like they understand.

Teenagers I
Their mouths grow in disproportion to their height.

Teenagers II
If a teenager can get lost, he or she will.

Telephones I

The telephone will ring when you are outside the door fumbling for the keys.

Telephones II

You will reach the phone just in time to hear the caller hanging up.

Telephoning

If a phone rings more than six times it probably won't be answered.

Theft

To steal from one person is plagiarism; to steal from many is research.

The terminally ill
Terminally ill people are more likely to die after a holiday than before.

Toddlers
They will never tell you that they need to go to the toilet until you have already put on their boots, mittens, coat, snow suit and hat.

Toilets
If you find ants around a toilet, it has probably just been used by a diabetic.

Trust

Trust only those who stand to lose as much as you when things go wrong.

Vomit

No child ever vomits in the bathroom.

Warm hearts

In marriage, a warm heart seldom makes up for cold hands.

Weddings
The length of a marriage is inversely proportional to the amount spent on the wedding.

Wives
Women who apologize to keep the peace, get divorced for constantly apologizing.

Women
Whatever women do, they must do twice as well as men to be thought half as good. Luckily, this is not difficult.

Wrong numbers

A caller who dials the wrong number will always call a second time, generally once you have comfortably sat back down in your favorite chair.

Youth

Young men want to be faithful and are not; old men want to be faithless and cannot.

Chapter 3

ABOUT THE HOME

I like children. If they're properly cooked.

W. C. Fields

Appliances
If nobody uses it, there's a reason.

Assembling flat-packed furniture
The fact that the label on a box claims that you need no tools has no bearing on whether you will actually need them.

Baby clothes
Giving away baby clothes and nursery furniture is a major cause of pregnancy.

Bags of rubbish

Bags of rubbish leaning against the wall will always fall towards you (and split open).

Baking biscuits

Never bother to bake biscuits – the children will only eat them.

Bar codes

The bar code at the till will never work for the items you are most embarrassed about buying.

Bills

No matter which utility company sends you a bill, the envelope they provide to return it in will always be shorter than the bill.

Blocked toilets

Blocked toilets are usually caused by excessive use of toilet paper. The best way to clear the blockage is with a plunger.

Boys' parties

Any birthday party of more than five male children under the age of thirteen will invariably end up in a fight.

Breaking plates

The plate you break will never be the one that was chipped already.

Building a fireplace

The flue area of a fireplace should be equal to or slightly greater than one-tenth of the area of the fireplace opening.

Burning coal

A pound of coal will provide slightly more than twice as much heat as a pound of wood.

Buses

A bus that has not arrived will do so only when the potential passenger has walked to a point so close to the destination that it is no longer worthwhile boarding the bus.

Buying artichokes
Fresh artichokes squeak when rubbed together.

Buying bananas
If you buy bananas before they are ripe there won't be
any left by the time they are ripe. If you buy them ripe
they will rot before you have a chance to eat them.

Buying Brussels sprouts
Never buy sprouts before the first frost.

Buying a dog
If a dog tolerates gentle handling between its toes, it is probably suitable for young children.

Buying food (general)
Shopping for groceries while hungry will triple the cost of the trip.

Buying fresh produce
In a well-run retail store, the fresh items come from the back of the shelf.

Buying glasses

When trying on glasses, put them on and look at your feet. If they start to slip off your face, then they are too loose.

Buying a hand tool

Never buy a hand tool that does not have the manufacturer's name permanently inscribed on it. The absence of a name indicates poor quality.

Buying a honeydew melon

A honeydew melon is ripe if the end opposite the stem gives easily when you press it with your thumb. When you rub the skin with your finger, it should also feel slightly sticky.

Buying a house I

The house you want is always more than the house you can afford.

Buying a house II

You've found the right house if, on your first visit, you can immediately visualize yourself and your family engaged in your regular activities among your current possessions. If you have to stop and think about how you would use each area or what furniture you would buy then forget it.

Buying a leather jacket

Leather that has been exposed to smoke won't stiffen after getting wet. The longer the leather has been smoked for, the darker it will become.

Buying lobster

A lobster tail should always curl. If this does not happen, the lobster is dead or dying. If the tail does not curl on a boiled lobster, the lobster was dead before it was boiled.

Buying a mattress

The amount you move during the night is directly proportional to the hardness of your mattress. Generally the greater the back problem, the harder your mattress should be. The unforgiving surface forces you to move often and your muscles won't become stiff from lack of movement.

Buying meat
If there is blood in a package of supermarket meat, the piece is less than fresh.

Buying pears
A pear is ripe when the flesh near the stem yields slightly to thumb pressure.

Buying a replacement
If you buy a new one, the old one will turn up immediately.

Buying shoes

You should have thumb's width of space between the longest toe and the tip of your shoe.

Buying a toothbrush

Get a new toothbrush as soon as your old one gets frayed. You should get through a toothbrush every three months.

Buying trainers

To decide how much money to spend on a pair of trainers, take the number of miles you run each week and multiply it by four.

Calling for help

If you are assaulted always shout out "Fire!" People are much more likely to come to your aid than if your shout "Help!"

Car boot sales

Always hold a car boot sale on the first Sunday of every month. People who get paid monthly will have most time and money on this day.

Car incidents

There will be no witnesses when a car backs into yours when you aren't there. There will be multiple witnesses when you back into someone else's car.

Cards
In a household with children, any deck of playing cards will have between thirty-eight and fifty-one cards.

Carpets
There is no such thing as a carpet that doesn't show dirt.

Changing your oil
Rub a little of your motor oil between your thumb and forefinger. If you feel any grit, it's time to change your oil.

Checking an egg
When placed in a bowl of water, a fresh egg will wink and lie on its side. An egg that's not fresh but still edible will sink and stand partially erect on its tapered end. A rotten egg will float.

Checking a nursing home
If you can smell urine when you enter the building, then don't put your granny there.

Checking pearls
To tell if a pearl is genuine, rub it against your teeth. A fake pearl will feel smooth, the real thing will grate.

Checking for sunburn

Press an exposed part of the body with your finger. If the skin is white when you lift your finger, then come out of the sun now.

Checking your water supply

You can tell if your water is hard or soft by looking at your ice cubes. Hard-water cubes have a white spot in the centre where minerals congregate; soft-water cubes are uniformly cloudy.

Check-out tills

If you're in a hurry, never choose the express check-out till.

Children's parties
Any child's birthday party where the number of guests is more than the age of the child whose party it is, will end in disaster.

Children's shoes
Children aged two to ten outgrow their shoes every three months.

Choking
If a choking person can verbally request the Heimlich maneuver, he or she doesn't need it.

Choosing a house

The larger the house, the more places there are to lose things in.

Choosing a neighborhood

You will usually find the more affluent, attractive neighborhoods on the north and west sides of a city; the poorer and more crime-prone neighborhoods will, therefore, be on the south and east.

Christmas presents

The amount of time that a child plays with their Christmas present is exactly one-fifth of the time it took for the parents to assemble it.

Cleanliness
Cleanliness is next to impossible.

Computers I
A computer does what you tell it do, not what you want it to do.

Computers II
If you understand it, it's obsolete.

Construction
Cut it large and kick it into place.

Cooking I

Once a dish has gone wrong, anything you might add to rescue it will only make it worse.

Cooking II

You will always receive the greatest number of compliments for the dish that took the least amount of time to prepare.

Cooking III

The more time and energy you put into preparing a meal, the greater the chance that your guests will spend the entire evening discussing other meals that they have eaten.

Cooking ostrich eggs

One ostrich egg will serve twenty-four people for brunch.

Cooking rice

Use one handful of rice per person. Rest the tip of the index finger on top of the rice and add enough water to reach the first joint.

Cooking a steak

If you want a medium-rare steak, it should be as firm as the puffy area between your thumb and index finger. If you want your steak rarer, it should be softer; more done, harder.

Crawling

Any infant who can crawl will crawl towards the nearest available fragile item.

Creaking stairs

You may be able to alleviate the problem of creaking stairs by puffing talcum powder into the gaps.

DIY I

All DIY will inevitably take three times longer than you thought it would.

DIY II
No two identical parts are ever alike.

Dogs
No dog will ever knock a vase over unless there is water in it.

Eating potatoes
People will eat one and a half times as many mashed potatoes as they would if the same potatoes were baked.

Electricity

The commonest cause of faults in lights are loose connections.

~·¡♠.·~

Engines

It pays to turn off your car engine if it will be idle for more than one minute.

~·¡♠.·~

Exhaust fumes

Blue smoke from your exhaust may mean your car needs a complete overhaul. Black smoke normally means a maladjusted carburettor. Ignore white smoke if the engine is cold but if it continues after the engine has warmed up then you may have a leaking head gasket.

Feeding a cat
Feed your cat as much as it will eat in thirty minutes, twice a day.

Fertilizing trees
Most trees need about half a pound of nitrogen per inch of trunk diameter.

Finding soft porn
Two out of every three magazines tossed along roadsides will be pornographic.

Flat batteries

As long as you intend to make a journey of ten miles or more immediately after getting going, the alternator should recharge the battery enough to ensure the car starts next time.

Flying particles

A flying particle will hit the nearest eye.

Frozen food

On a package of frozen food, if it takes longer to read the ingredients than to cook it in a microwave, choose another product.

Fuses
Fuses never blow in daylight hours.

Futons
It takes two futons to make a comfortable bed.

Getting a loan
In order to get a loan you must first prove that you don't need it.

Good housekeeping
Every flat surface is a potential table.

Hammers
Anything hit with a big enough hammer will fall apart.

Heating by people
Ten people will raise the temperature of a medium-sized room by 1 degree per hour.

Houseflies
If you're more than three feet away from a housefly, it can't see you.

Houseplants
The life expectancy of a house plant varies inversely with its price and directly with its ugliness.

Inanimate objects
All inanimate objects can move just enough to get in your way.

Insurance
The fine print on all home insurance policies states that "this policy is void in case of a claim."

Juice

Do not pour any more juice for your child that the amount that you are prepared to wipe up.

Junk

Junk accumulates to fill the space available for it.

Ladders

When you use an extension ladder, you should put the bottom of the ladder one foot away from the wall for every four feet of vertical height.

Laundry

You should expect to lose one sock every time you do your laundry.

Looking up numbers

Whenever you need to look up a phone number you will only ever have the directory containing the other half of the alphabet.

Losing your purse

The day you lose your purse will be the day on which it has contained the most loose cash in ten years.

Lost property

There is a parallel universe containing all lost socks.

Maps
When you're trying to look something up on a map, the traffic lights will turn green as soon as you stop at them.

Maternity clothes
No woman can ever believe that she's going get that big. There will come a point when even the most expensive maternity dress will look utterly ridiculous.

Measuring snow
One inch of rain would make ten inches of snow.

Moving home

Each time you move, things are lost, broken or discarded. For the average family, six moves equal one house fire.

Multiple-function gadgets

Multiple-function gadgets will not perform any function adequately (and they take up a lot of room).

Nappies

Changing your baby's nappy will always cause the telephone to ring.

Neighborhood dogs
The volume of the neighbor's dog's bark is inversely proportional to the intelligence of its owner.

Noise
Scary noises intensify at night.

One size
"One size" normally means it won't fit.

Onion chopping
The number of tears in a man's eyes when he is chopping onions is directly in proportion to the number of ladies watching him.

Painting
Don't dip your paintbrush into the paint more than one-third to one-half the length of its exposed bristles.

Paper bags
No carrier bag can hold all the rubbish created by the groceries which were brought into the house within it.

Parenting

Let your children go if you want to keep them.

Parking

The distance you have to park from your home increases in direct proportion to the weight of the packages that you have to carry.

Personal finance

Your monthly mortgage payments should not exceed 28 per cent of your gross monthly salary.

Picking your raspberries

When you start to find garden spiders in your raspberries, you have one week left to pick them.

Plumbing

The least amount of effort exerted by a DIY enthusiast on his plumbing will produce the greatest volume of water.

Posting a letter

You remember to post a letter only when you're nowhere near a post box.

Preserving shoes

Shoes last twice as long if you keep them in their shoe box when you aren't wearing them.

Prints

Commercially produced art prints are never sized to fit commercially produced frames.

Pruning trees

When pruning a branch from a tree, never leave a stub long enough to hang your hat on.

Purchasing essential items

A necessary item will always go on sale the week after you purchased it at the regular price.

Rain I
If the birds are out in the rain, the rain will continue for the rest of the day.

Rain II
Rain before 7 a.m. done by 11 a.m.

Rain III
When trees start to show the whitish undersides of their leaves then it's about to rain.

Relocating property
Whenever you move an object to a more logical home, you will only ever be able to remember where it used to go.

Repair men
You can guarantee that if you have called out a repair man to fix your central heating at emergency rates on the evening of a public holiday, you will have forgotten to switch the system on.

Repairs – general
With a cheap radio or cassette player, it's probably not worth fixing if you can't fix it yourself within half-an-hour.

Replacing a fuse
If your car blows a fuse and you don't have a spare, one wrap of cigarette pack foil around the old fuse will give you a twenty-amp emergency fuse. Two wraps will give you about thirty-five amps.

Replacing a luxury item
If it's your favorite, they'll stop making it.

Roasting chicken (bizarrely)
To make sure your chicken is thoroughly roasted, mix a handful of uncooked popcorn with the stuffing. In roughly an hour, when the chicken explodes, the fragments will be tender and juicy.

Selecting food

The best oil is at the top; the best wine is in the middle; the best honey is on the bottom.

Selling a car

Your adored and utterly reliable car will never start first time when a potential purchaser turns up for a test drive.

Sending children to school

A child is old enough to go to school when he can cross his arms over his head and grasp his ears with his opposite hands.

Sending Christmas cards

You should receive at least two Christmas cards for every three you send.

Shelves

You will always have more books than shelves to put them on.

Shopping in sales

At a sale, the only dress you will want to buy is the one not in the sale.

Solutions

Every solution breeds new problems.

~ 🔔 ~

Starting the car

The amount of petrol consumed each time you switch on your ignition is the equivalent of ninety seconds spent in neutral.

~ 🔔 ~

Storage space

All storage space will eventually be taken up with objects that your children are saving for their children.

~ 🔔 ~

Straight lines

There is no such thing as a straight line.

Swatting flies

Wait for a fly to land. Clap your hands together one or two inches directly above the fly since flies always fly straight up first when making a getaway.

Tape

The same piece of tape that would not stick your child's drawing to the wall will never come off the fridge.

Telephone cord

Telephone cord only hangs freely and untwisted on television sets.

Throwing away clothes

Wait one year before throwing out a piece of clothing. If you haven't worn it for a whole year, you'll never wear it again.

Throwing away things

The average time between throwing something away and needing that object is two weeks – less if it is needed urgently.

Time-saving gadgets

The time saved by using a time-saving gadget is the amount of time required to clean and service it.

Toddlers

A toddler will learn to say "nanny," ten minutes after she has left her grandparents' house.

Tools I

Any tool when dropped will automatically roll into the least accessible corner of the workshop – unless it lands on your toes first.

Tools II

If it can break, it will, but only after the guarantee has run out.

Toothpaste
There is always one more squeeze in the toothpaste.

Toys I
An unbreakable toy is most useful for breaking other toys.

Toys II
No toy that you ever buy your child will ever interest them for more than half an hour. Every toy that every other parent buys for every other child will interest your child endlessly.

Toys III

The more expensive the toy, the greater the tendency for the child to play with the box.

Tree roots

You can assume that the roots of normally shaped trees extend at least to the drip line of the branches.

Tying shoelaces

If one shoelace is loose, you need to retie both.

Unwatched pots

An unwatched pot will boil immediately.

Wallets

Never leave your wallet on the roof of the car. You will inevitably drive off having forgotten that you put it there.

Washing

Anything small enough to fit into a trouser pocket will eventually end up in the washing machine.

Washing up

When you have completely finished the washing-up, there is always one more piece of loose cutlery left in the bottom of the sink.

Watering your houseplants
When in doubt, don't. For plants on you patio or windowsill, however, when in doubt, do.

Watering the lawn
It's time to water your lawn when the grass has a purplish cast and when footprints remain after walking across the lawn – which is a sign of wilting.

Waterproof clothes
Do not exist.

Wedding presents

Wedding presents always come in pairs – two toasters, two juicers, two coffee percolators.

Wire coat-hangers

Wire coat-hangers always multiply in dark wardrobes.

Workshops

The least expensive but most important item needed for a DIY project will always be forgotten.

Yellow pages

Anything you look for in the yellow pages will not be listed in the category you first tried. Try the third category that springs to mind first.

Chapter 4

ABOUT WORK

It's true hard work never killed anybody, but I figure why take the chance?

Ronald Reagan

Acting
Whatever happens, look as if it were intended.

Appearances
Never walk down a hallway in an office building without a piece of paper in your hand.

Approximations
An easily understood, workable approximation is more useful than a complex, incomprehensible truth.

Artists
The overwhelming prerequisite for the greatness of an artist is that artist's death.

Attending job interviews I

Never spend more than sixty seconds answering a question. In your first interview never ask about holidays, pay or pensions, this will only give the impression that you are looking for an easy job. First get an offer and then state your terms.

Attending job interviews II

Always schedule the first interviews for the jobs you care about least. The experience will only enhance your performance at the interviews you care about most.

Avoiding errors I
If a variety of things that could have gone wrong did not go wrong then it would have been ultimately beneficial for them to have gone wrong.

Avoiding errors II
Two wrongs are only the beginning.

Bad news
The sooner you announce bad news, the better.

Bureaucracy
A bureaucracy can outwait anything.

Boss

The boss who attempts to impress employees with his knowledge of intricate details has lost sight of his final objective.

Business travel

The distance to the gate is inversely proportional to the time available to catch your flight.

Buying a computer

Every two years you can buy a computer that performs twice as well for half the price.

Catching a pyromaniac

A pyromaniac is proud of his work and will be found in the crowd watching the fire.

Catching an arsonist

A professional arsonist will be somewhere else, establishing an alibi.

Celebrities

A celebrity is a person who works hard all his life to become well known and then wears dark glasses to avoid being recognized.

Company names
The longer the name, the smaller the company.

Deadline
The deadline is one week after the original deadline.

Delegating I
Never make a decision that somebody else can make for you. The first rule of leadership is to save yourself for the big decisions. In any group meetings, the person doing the least talking is the one with the most power.

Delegating II
Never give an employee a project after 4.30 p.m. unless it can be completed by 5 p.m.

Designing billboards
People are exposed to outdoor advertisements for only a few seconds. A good billboard should have no more than seven words and two things to look at on it.

Campaigning

For every person who gets involved in your campaign by contributing money, putting up a poster or distributing literature, expect ten to fifteen votes on election day. While money doesn't guarantee a victory, the lack of money guarantees a loss.

Canvassing

When you are canvassing door-to-door you can optimise your "time per voter" by spending no more than twenty to thirty seconds with each person you meet. Most people will decide whether they like you within that time and most will want to get back to whatever they were doing before you interrupted them. You should, however, take time to discuss issues with the interested persons.

Catching shoplifters
Shoplifters are most active on Fridays and Sundays between 3 p.m. and 6 p.m.

Colleagues
It's difficult to soar with eagles when you work with turkeys.

Comics
It's easy to be a comic when you have the whole government working for you.

Committees

A committee is a group of twelve people doing the work of one.

Completion

It's amazing how long it takes to complete something you are not working on.

Conferences I

Any simple problem can be made insoluble if enough conferences are held to discuss it.

Conferences II

The only two interesting lectures will be held at the same time.

Consultants

Consultants are elusive men and women in expensive suits who ask a company for a number and then give it back to them.

Consulting

A consultant should never charge for less than half a day of work.

Contacts

The inside contact that you have spent great time and expense cultivating is the first person to be made redundant in a reorganization.

Cooperatives
A cooperative effort loses effectiveness when it includes more than fifteen people.

Copying data
Always make a copy of everything on your computer. If it's really important, make two.

Copying information
If something is confidential, it will be left in the photocopying machine.

Correcting a teacher
If a teacher says, "Please correct me if I make a mistake" do it once and once only.

Critics
Critics are like eunuchs in a harem: they know how it's done, they've seen it done every day, but they're unable to do it themselves.

Customer relations
The client who pays the least, complains the most.

Decision making

Eighty per cent of bad decisions are snap decisions. Good managers make the best decisions after sleeping on the matter.

Democracy

Democracy is the worst form of government except all the other forms that have been tried from time to time.

Designing a chair

If you're designing a chair and want to know how well it will stand the test of time, then imagine thirty of them lined up in a launderette.

Designing a city street

A city street is most visually appealing if its width is the same as the height of the buildings along it.

Designing a supermarket

Supermarket efficiency increases with store size to a maximum of 22,000 square feet. After that, economies of scale are offset by communication problems.

Digging a grave

When digging a grave by hand, haul away seventeen wheelbarrow-loads of dirt and pile the rest by the hole. You will have just the right amount to fill the grave.

Diplomacy
A diplomat is a man who thinks twice before he says nothing.

Discoveries
All great discoveries are made by mistake.

Editing fiction
An author's willingness to allow his prose to be edited is inversely proportional to its need to be edited.

Employing people

A corporation should limit its executive staff to one hundred people or less, even though it may have thousands of employees. In half of all cases, when an employee calls in sick, he or she really is sick. No manager should have responsibility for more than six separate activities.

Exams – essays

Answer an essay question as if you were talking to your parents. The closer you are to running out of time, the less you should fiddle with your answers.

Exams – multiple choice

In a multiple-choice situation, never change your first guess – it is always the best. When in doubt, always pick D on a multiple-choice test.

Exams – revision I
The less time you took to remember something, the quicker you will forget it.

Exams – revision II
The more studying you did for an exam, the less able you will be to decide which question to answer when you're actually taking it.

Expenses
No matter how many employees share a taxi and no matter who pays, each will claim the full fare on his expense account.

Expert advice
If you consult enough experts you can confirm any opinion.

Explaining computers

When explaining a computer command, a computer language feature or a piece of computer hardware, first describe the problem it is designed to solve.

Explaining ideas

If you can't explain the idea to a ten-year-old then you don't understand it yourself.

Experts

Even when all the experts agree, they may well be wrong.

Failure
When all else fails, try the boss's suggestion.

Failure in mathematics
If you're not famous in the field of mathematics by the time you're twenty-two, you probably never will be.

Female executives
Any successful businesswoman is assumed to henpeck her husband.

Fighting guerrillas

To fight a guerrilla army, a national army needs ten soldiers for every guerrilla.

Filing

If you file it, you'll know where it is but never need it. If you don't file it, you'll need it but never know where it is.

Film industry

If the producer and the director of a film don't hate each other, then don't invest money in it.

Foreign affairs
The further your readership is from the facts of a situation, the more likely they are to believe what you write about it.

Free time
Free time which unexpectedly becomes available will be wasted.

Freelancing
When invoicing for freelance work, always figure out what you think you can get away with charging and then double it. In 90 per cent of cases you will get what you ask, in 100 per cent the final expense and aggravation will exceed your original estimate in any event.

Handling stolen paintings
A stolen painting will sell for one tenth of what it would sell for on the open market.

Hierarchies I
The cream rises to the top. So does the scum.

Hierarchies II
The only important information in a hierarchy is who knows what.

Hollywood

Hollywood is a place where they shoot too many movies and not enough actors.

Hosting a talk show

During a radio talk show, at least 1 per cent of the callers will phone in simply to tell you how hard it was to get through to the show.

Illness at work

The number of minor illnesses among the employees is inversely proportional to the health of the organization.

Insider trading

If an investor even suspects that a share tip is based on insider information and the share price would be affected if the public knew about it, then it is probably an illegal deal.

Insurance fraud

To determine the true value of items stolen in a burglary, take the reported value and divide by three.

Interrupters

The one who says it cannot be done should never interrupt the one who is doing it.

Invigilators

If class attendance is mandatory, an exam will produce increased absenteeism. If attendance is optional, an exam will produce students you have never before set eyes on.

Job conditions

The more you need your job for financial reasons, the worse you will be treated.

Job titles

The longer your job title and description, the less important you are in the hierarchy.

Journalism

The further away the disaster or accident occurs, the greater the number of dead and injured required for it to become a news story.

Keeping your retail customers I

For every complaint a company receives, there are twenty-six other customers with problems and six are serious. Between 54 and 70 per cent of customers who complain to a company will do business with the company again if their complaint was resolved. The figure increases to 95 per cent if the customer feels the complaint was resolved quickly.

Keeping your retail customers II
If you get rid of the 20 per cent of your customers who cause 80 per cent of the headaches, your profits will increase by 30 per cent.

Law
Bad law is more likely to be supplemented than repealed.

Lecturing in Bulgaria
When lecturing in Bulgaria, write twenty minutes of material for a sixty-minute speech to allow sufficient time for translation.

Looking at specks on paper
If your eyes can see it, you need to worry about it.

Looking good on TV
Always try to match the colour of your make-up to the colour of the tip of your tongue.

Losing weight
The best way to lose weight is to eat less.

Lunchtime

The man who spends his lunchtime in bars and restaurants with his mates is Making Useful Contacts. The woman who spends her lunchtime nipping home to check on her children is considered to be lacking in commitment to her job.

Making milk

A cow needs about three pounds of water to make a pound of milk.

Making a speech

Allow an hour and a half of research, thinking and writing for every minute of a speech. Expect the speech to take one-third longer than it took you in rehearsal.

Managers

Anyone can make a decision given enough facts. A good manager can make a decision without enough facts. A perfect manager can operate in perfect ignorance.

Manufacturing silk

It takes 110 silkworm cocoons to make a tie and 630 to make a shirt.

Mathematics

Nobody wants to read anyone else's formulae.

Measuring

The first joint of your thumb measures about one inch, your foot measures about one foot and your nose measures about one yard.

~◦❦◦~

Mess

A magazine that travels thousands of miles in the post will wait until it falls through your letterbox to drop all its loose subscription cards on the floor.

~◦❦◦~

Negotiating a deal

When negotiating, always use a deadline. Ninety per cent of the agreement will come in the last 10 per cent of the time allotted.

New clients

A job with a new client will take 25 per cent longer than the same job with an established client.

Obeying orders

If you are given two contradictory orders, obey them both.

Organizations I

In any organization there will always be one person who knows what is going on.

Organizations II

Every organization has an allotted number of positions to be filled by misfits.

Organizing property viewings

Unless you get a name and phone number, half of all people who make appointments to view properties won't show up.

Packing up a rock band

If you are in a four-piece band it takes about eight hours to pack up your equipment, travel to your local gig, unload, set up, play one set, break down, load up and return home. Add one half-hour for each additional piece and add one hour for each additional set played.

Painting a motorway

A road must carry traffic of at least four hundred cars per day for a reflective centre line to be a cost-effective improvement.

Placing an ad

When placing an advertisement in a magazine, the first right-hand page and the back cover are the best places. These are followed by over-cover positions and the front section. Never place your ad in the back of a magazine if you can help it.

Planning an advertising campaign

To attract women, show babies and women. To attract men, show men. The visual part of a television commercial accounts for 85 per cent of the impact on the viewer; the soundtrack accounts for 15 per cent.

Planning a car park

If you are designing a parking space, count on three hundred square feet per vehicle.

Planning a meeting

A meeting without an agenda will take twice as long and accomplish half as much as a meeting with an agenda.

Planning permission

Permission will only be granted when none of the councillors can be blamed if the project fails but when all of the councillors can claim credit if it succeeds.

Political campaigns

Candidates with strong, aggressive personalities and specific "programs" get elected half as often as accommodating, compromising candidates who are interesting persons and want to provide "constituent services."

Political success

All political success is based on the indifference of the majority.

Politics

To succeed in politics, it is often necessary to rise above your principles.

Press conferences
The explanation of a disaster will be made by a stand-in.

Principles of business
Marketing says yes. Finance says no.

Proofreading
If you find one error while proofreading, there are likely to be several more in the same or contiguous paragraphs.

Publishing

If you ask a publisher if a new book is doing well and they reply "it's too soon to tell," then it isn't.

Raising a hand

When a teacher needs someone to volunteer an answer, raise your hand at the same time as the class genius. If you time it correctly, neither of you will ever be picked.

Raising money

University fund-raisers plan on getting one-third of their money from ten big contributors, one-third from one hundred medium contributors and one-third from everyone else.

Raising pigs

When a sow conceives, make a notch just above the moon on your fingernail. When this mark grows off the end of the nail, the sow is about to give birth.

Receiving tips

The most generous tippers are men out on dates with women who aren't their wives.

Recognizing the obvious

Clients will recognize the obvious much sooner than professionals.

Recruitment I

Foreign talent always seems more talented than your in-house deputy. The truth is probably the other way around.

Recruitment II

If you are checking a reference and you ask someone's former employer, "would you hire this person again?" any answer except "yes" is a "no."

Renting property

The market value of a rental property is six times the gross rent.

Repeating an experiment
If you can't repeat your own experiment, you are probably wrong. If no one else can repeat your experiment, you are probably lying.

Representing an author
Any author who begins a letter to an agent with the words "My name is . . ." should not be seriously considered.

Research
The more trivial your research, the more people will read it and agree.

Rubbish bins/garbage

You have to look through a wastepaper basket three times to find any missing piece of paper.

Running an air force

American, German and British forces expect to have 40 per cent of their aircraft under repair at any given time.

Running a bookstore

If you stock six of any book, you'll sell three in one week, two more in one month and still have the final one when you eventually retire. Ten per cent of bookstore customers buy 90 per cent of the books. Ten per cent never buy anything.

Running a newspaper

A magazine or newspaper needs to receive about 50 per cent of its revenue from advertising to survive financially.

Running a parking firm

Most cities expect the annual income from parking meter fines to be twice the income from parking meter payments.

Running a restaurant

If a customer likes your restaurant, he'll tell two other people. If a customer hates your restaurant, he'll tell seven other people.

Sackings
The last person to have been sacked or to have left will be blamed for everything that goes wrong.

Science
If it's green or it wriggles, it's biology.
If it stinks, it's chemistry.
If it doesn't work, it's physics.

Secretaries
The secretary who decides to gulp down a quick sandwich at her desk for lunch is the one deemed to be available for emergency dictation.

Selling cigarettes
One out of ten cigarette smokers changes brands annually.

Selling to the elderly
Elderly consumers think that they are fifteen years younger than they actually are.

Selling in person
When greeting a customer, make sure your first remark refers directly to the product that you are hoping to sell. The sale is made while the customer is talking. After knocking on a door, always stand at least four feet back from the door.

Selling by post

The average response to a mail-shot is two replies for every hundred pieces of mail. The response to a direct-mail campaign peaks one week to ten days after you receive the first reply. The best months to sell something by mail-order are September and January.

Selling by telephone

Always let the customer hang up first. Jumping the gun means you might miss a last-minute order.

Shearing a sheep

You can plan on making one sweater for every two pounds of wool you shear from a sheep.

Shooting at helicopters

If an airplane or helicopter is bigger than your thumb when held at arm's length then you can bring it down with hand-held weapons.

Sitting down

People who work sitting down always get paid more than those who work standing up.

Slogans

A good slogan can stop analysis for five years.

Sneaking in

Office machines which function perfectly in normal working hours will break down when you return to the office at night to use them for private business.

Sorting out papers

All papers below the top one are upside down or the wrong way round until you correct this. Then the process repeats itself.

Spare parts

If you need a spare part, buy two. The chances are that you will need it again one day. But never buy a new piece of equipment unless it can pay for itself within three months.

Speeches
It normally takes three weeks to prepare a good impromptu speech.

Starting a business
Never start a new business unless you can afford to wait for at least a year before you begin to make a profit.

Starting a cattle ranch
When setting up a cattle ranch, always start with the same breed of cattle as your neighbors. Specialize later when you've got a bit more experience.

Stud location

If you need to locate a stud in a stick-framed wall, remember that most electricians are right-handed. Find an outlet and tap the wall directly to its left. The odds are in your favour that the stud will be there and you can measure away from it in sixteen-inch increments to find other studs.

Superiors

Never let your superiors know that you know more than them.

Supervisors

The one moment in the day when you lean back and relax will be the precise second that your supervisor walks past.

Suppliers
All suppliers of parts needed urgently over the weekend will only ever be open for business during the week.

Talking to journalists
Never tell a journalist anything you wouldn't want to see in print. They may be trustworthy but their friends might not be.

Teaching I
No one is listening until you make a mistake.

Teaching II

For effective teaching, a class should be limited to twenty-five students.

Teaching III

Never turn your back on the class. This is what overhead projectors were invented for.

Technology

Any technical problem can be overcome given enough time and money.

Treating a household pet

The owner of a dog or cat that bites the vet can be guaranteed to say "he's never done that before."

Trends
When in doubt predict that the trend will continue.

Typing
A full, double-spaced typewritten page will consist of about 250 words.

Using a long word
If you're writing an article and you need to look up a word in the dictionary, you probably shouldn't be using it.

Watching a takeover
When a company is taken over by another firm in the same field and it was doing well before the takeover, it will do less well afterwards. If it was not doing well before the takeover, its future will be about as murky as before – or a little more so.

Women

If a woman is told her work is indispensable, it usually means she's going to carry on being underpaid.

Working in the army

If it moves, salute it. If it doesn't, paint it.

Working with dynamite

Wait at least an hour before investigating any charge of dynamite that didn't go off.

Working in a library

Twenty per cent of a library's patrons account for 80 per cent of the library's use. Twenty per cent of the books in a library account for 80 per cent of the library's use.

Working with parishioners

The first year they love you, the second year they hate you, the third year they understand you.

Working on a submarine

If you work on a submarine always add the number of times you have descended to the number of times you have surfaced and divide the total by two. If there is one left over, don't open the hatch.

Writing an advertisement

Always use sentences of less than twelve words.

Writing an autobiography

An autobiography is an obituary in serial form with the last paragraph missing.

Writing a manual I

It is a simple task to make things complex, but a complex task to make them simple.

Writing a manual II

When a writer compiles a manual on a topic she does not understand, her work will be understood only by those readers who know more about the subject than she does.

Writing a sports book

The sales success of a sports book is inversely proportional to the size of the ball used in the sport.

Chapter 5

ABOUT LEISURE

You're not drunk if you can lie on the floor
without holding on.

Dean Martin

Adventure
Adventure is rarely fun while it's happening.

Alcohol absorption
Traces of alcohol remain in the body for forty-eight hours.

Arranging flowers
A flower arrangement should usually be about one and a half times the height or width of the container.

Backpacking
All trails have more uphill sections than level or downhill sections.

Baggage in hall
Wherever you position yourself around the carousel, your baggage will always come out last.

Bedtime stories
You cannot underestimate a child's capacity for repetition.

Best man's speech
A best man's speech should be just like a fashionable dress: long enough to cover the subject but short enough to be interesting.

Betting
Never bet on a loser because you think his luck is bound to change.

Betting on a horse
If you don't know any of the horses in a race, bet on the one with the thinnest waist.

Bird watching
The smaller the bird, the closer it will allow you to approach. The single best clue to a bird's identity is the shape of its bill.

Brick ovens

A brick oven is ready to use when the bricks all look red. If the black spots are not all burned off, then the oven isn't hot enough. If you sprinkle flour on the hearth and it turns black instantly then the oven is too hot.

Building an igloo

An igloo should be built in an area where the snow is packed just loose enough to make a footprint, but not so loose that a footprint blows away in a high wind.

Buying art

Paintings in galleries sell for twice the price they raise at auction.

Buying books
Never judge a book by its cover price.

Buying a camera
You should buy the simplest camera in the highest price range you can justify.

Buying a car
The best time to buy a new car is the last day of the month because most car sales staff are on commission and want their monthly reports to look good. They will, therefore, be most likely to bargain on this day. You can increase your chances of getting a good deal by choosing the youngest salesperson on the floor.

Buying a car stereo

The sound you hear from a car stereo system is made by the speakers, not the tape deck. Your speakers should never cost less than two-thirds of the price of the rest of the equipment.

Buying cheese for a party

For a wine and cheese party, count on one pound of cheese for every five guests.

Buying clothes I

A garment is probably well made if strips or tweeds are matched at the seams. The more seams that match, the better the garment. You can check the length of a jacket with your arms relaxed at your sides. The hem of the jacket should reach the tip of your thumbs.

Buying clothes II

If you have to convince yourself that you need a particular item of clothing then don't buy it – you'll be adding another dust collector to your wardrobe.

Buying a horse

The cheapest time of year to buy a horse is fall.

Cakes
Children prefer cakes that have gone wrong.

Camping
A camping trip is in jeopardy whenever early risers or night owls exceed 50 per cent of the party. If either is a majority, the other campers should reassess their plans.

Casserole
A casserole can progress from uncooked to burned without passing through singe.

Catching fish

Fish are feeding actively only 5 to 10 per cent of the time. The rest of the time they are either in a neutral feeding mood (80 per cent) or a negative one (10 per cent).

Champagne

When serving champagne, if you give a half-twist to the bottle at the top of the glass, this will prevent the champagne from bubbling over the rim.

Checking a drawing

It's easier to check the proportions of a drawing if it's held upside down.

Checking wind when flying a plane

If you're in an airplane and you can't find any flags to indicate the wind direction on the ground, check the way the cows are facing. Cows prefer to face away from the wind when they're grazing and when they're lying on the ground chewing their cud.

Cheese

The more varied the selection of cheeses you serve, the fewer varieties your guests will try.

Choosing a car color
One out of every ten new cars sold is white, the most popular color. It is also the safest — the average pedestrian will spot a white car twelve times more quickly than a black one. When buying a new car, choose the same color that the manufacturer has used in the adverts for that particular car since this is the one most likely to also grab a secondhand buyer's eye.

Choosing a cruise ship
The longer and more expensive the cruise, the older the average age of the passengers.

Choosing a gambling partner
You will almost always gamble better if you gamble alone.

Choosing a restaurant abroad

When traveling in a foreign country, avoid restaurants with menus printed in more than one language – they are for tourists.

Choosing a tennis racket I

If your tennis racket twists in your hand, the grip is probably too small. If your arm tires from hanging on too tightly, the grip is too big.

Choosing a tennis racket II

To choose the right grip for a tennis racket, measure the distance from the tip of your middle finger to the crease in the middle of your palm. That equals the right size handle.

Classics

A classic book is one which everybody praises but nobody reads.

Classical music

If a piece of classical music was written after you were born, you are not obliged to like it.

Climbing aboard a boat

If there are three or more inches of water in the bilge of a rowing boat, don't get in. Your weight will be enough to capsize the boat.

Climbing Mount Everest
The death rate for climbers on Mount Everest is one for every seven to make it to the top. The rate is lower for Sherpas and women and higher for military people.

Cocktail parties
Cocktail parties are a device for paying off obligations to people you don't want to invite to dinner.

Comparing films to the novel
The one created first will be better. The sequel will always be worse.

Cooking with an open fire
Use flames for boiling and baking; coals for frying.

Cooking outdoors
Melting snow for water or cooking outside a tent requires twice as much fuel as cooking inside a tent.

Cooking spaghetti
When spaghetti is done, it will stick to the wall.

Culture shock
Culture shock occurs only in the first three foreign countries you visit on any one trip. After that, you automatically focus on similarities rather than differences.

Deep water

To find the deepest water in a river, look for the middle of the inverted V of glossy water where the main current flows. At a bend in a river, the water is deepest on the outside of the turn.

Dinner guests

The parents of one child find a baby-sitter. The parents of four always bring their children with them.

Diving

A face mask for diving fits properly if you can hold it on your face, out of the water, with nothing but the suction from your nose.

Dog fights

If two dogs are headed for a fight and they appear about evenly matched, the dog on his home turf will win easily.

Dressing for skiing

When cross-country skiing, if you are warm when you first walk outside, you're wearing too much.

Driving alone

When you're driving alone at night, resist the temptation to rely on one long nap in the middle of the journey. Instead, take two short naps, with an hour of driving in between. This maximizes the amount of deep sleep per driving time.

Driving on ice and snow

Second gear is the best one for driving on ice and snow.

Driving in mountains

When driving in the mountains, brake before you reach a curve, then accelerate as you drive into the curve. You should always be able to stop in the distance you can see.

Driving a racing car

If a track is new to you, always use a higher gear than you think you're going to need in a turn. This will help prevent you from over-revving on a corner that surprises you and may keep you from doing something embarrassing.

Drunk drivers

On Friday and Saturday nights, one in ten cars coming towards you has a drunk driver behind the wheel.

Entertaining the elderly

Older people are consistently early arrivals. If you plan a luncheon for twelve thirty, expect all the retired people to arrive by noon.

Evening classes I

The more general the title of the course, the less you will learn from it.

Evening classes II

The less good-looking your fellow students, the less likely you are to turn up for lesson two.

Exercising

Never exercise so hard that you are gasping for breath. In fact, never do anything so hard that you are gasping for breath.

Exploring a cave

Always have at least four people on any caving expedition. If someone gets injured, two people can go for help while one stays with the injured party. This way no one has to remain in the cave alone.

Fashion

No woman will ever admit to having worn the same outfit as the absurdly clad heroine of a film which her teenage daughter is currently ridiculing.

Fishing

The least experienced fisherman always catches the biggest fish.

Fishing with a barometer
The lower the barometer, the better the fishing.

Flower arranging
Put into the vase one-third as many flowers as you think you need, then take half of them out again.

Flying I
As soon as the air hostess serves the coffee, the airplane will encounter turbulence.

Flying II
It takes your body one day to adjust to each time zone you cross.

Following deer

If deer droppings are black, moist and glossy the deer left them within fifteen or twenty minutes and is in the immediate vicinity. If the droppings are no longer glossy, they have been on the ground for an hour or more and the deer is probably bedded down on a southern slope. Gray deer droppings were left the previous day.

Football

Nothing is ever so bad that it can't be made worse by firing your coach.

Four-wheel drive
Four-wheel drive just means getting stuck in more inaccessible places.

French
French speakers use twice as many syllables per sentence as English speakers.

Giving presents
However many scraps of wrapping paper you save, you will never have the right amount to wrap a present in a hurry.

Going to bed with your cat
Generally speaking if your cat nudges your feet in the morning, it wants to stay inside. If it nudges your face, it wants to go out.

Golf balls

When looking for lost golf balls first try ten yards past the spot where you thought the ball landed.

Guitar strings

The first string that breaks on a guitar is usually the high E. The next most likely to break is the G string.

Hairdressing

Hairdressers will always assume that stunned horror is, in fact, ecstasy.

Heavy seas
On a yacht, when it looks like the wind conditions are about to degenerate, the canvas should be reduced as soon as you think it seems to be a good idea.

Hitching a lift
The more graffiti there is on the back of a road sign, the harder it will be to hitch a ride standing next to it.

Hobbies
After you have purchased the most expensive piece of equipment that your hobby requires, you will go off the hobby entirely.

Hotel selection on the basis of risk

Pick a hotel room between the third and sixth floors. Three floors puts you above street attacks and random shootings while six floors is low enough for a fireman's ladder to reach if the hotel catches fire.

Inking a rubber stamp

The finer the detail on a rubber stamp, the less ink it takes and the easier it is to get a good impression.

Jam-making

When making jam from all the free strawberries that your neighbor has kindly given you after a day out in Hampshire, remember to factor in the cost of redecorating the kitchen.

Keeping a cow
The average cow needs two acres of good pasture.

Keeping horses
A horse with a dull coat needs more corn in its diet.

Kite flying I
A kite automatically assumes its own best height. It is difficult, if not impossible, to alter this position. If you carry on letting out string after this point, the kite will merely move longitudinally away from you and will therefore merely be lower.

Kite flying II
There is never the right amount of wind to fly a kite.

Lightning I
During an electrical storm, if the hair on your arms and head starts to stand on end, lightning is going to strike near you. Drop to your knees and bend forward, putting your hands on your knees. Don't place your hand on the ground or you will be vulnerable to ground current if a lightning bolt hits within fifty yards.

Lightning II
For every second's pause between the appearance of lightning and the hearing of thunder, the storm is one mile away.

Literature
Works of literature tend to be about having sex and not about having children. Life tends to be the other way around.

Locker rooms
In an otherwise empty locker room, any two individuals will have adjoining lockers.

Magazine covers
The part of the magazine cover that you really want to look at is always covered by the address label.

Making bread

To test your bread dough, poke two holes in it as deeply as the first joint of your thumb. If the holes are still there after thirty seconds, it has risen enough.

Making coffee

A pound and a half of ground coffee will make ninety cups of decent coffee.

Making a serving dish

To make a ceramic serving dish, casserole, or bean pot, use one pound of clay for each person you want the pot to serve. For example, five pounds of clay will make a dish that will serve five people, with second helpings for some.

Model kits

Experienced modelers routinely scavenge parts from old kits or combine one kit with another. Don't try to match up model kits with more than a 20 per cent difference in scale unless you're prepared to do an awful lot of modification.

Mountain climbing

The peak looks closer than it is.

Musicals

You can tell how bad a musical is by how many times the chorus yells, "Hurrah."

Orchestras

The important thing is to start together and finish together. This will cover up a multitude of faults in between.

Ordering at a Chinese restaurant

When you order Chinese food for a group, always choose one dish less than you think you need.

Ordering at a vegetarian restaurant

Don't order anything at a vegetarian restaurant that would have meat in it if served elsewhere.

Organizing a party

Never invite a determined raconteur to a party to be held in a room of less than 600 square feet, not counting the piano. Otherwise the only way for your other guests to avoid him will be to leave the party.

Overeating

The first time that it occurs to you that you have eaten enough, you have.

Overtaking

You can safely overtake the car in front when you can see its headlights in your inside rear-view mirror.

Parties

The only parties a person regrets are the ones they didn't go to.

Photographing a car

A three-quarter front view makes the most effective photograph for selling a car.

Planning a party

If you invite one hundred people to a cocktail party, seventy-five will turn up.

Planning a wedding

Everyone knows at least 250 people well enough to invite to their wedding. You need two ushers for every fifty wedding guests.

Planting bulbs

If you're not sure how deeply you should plant a flower bulb, then try three times its length.

Planting seeds

Never plant a seed deeper than twice its width.

Playgrounds

The child on the swing will want the slide. The child on the slide will want the climbing frame. The child on the climbing frame will fall off.

Playing tennis with a partner

Whenever your partner comes over to your side of the court and shouts "I've got it," you can be sure that they have not.

Poetry

All bad poetry springs from sincere emotion.

Poison

Any plant with white sap is probably poisonous.

Rambling
Most well-trodden paths lead nowhere.

Renting a video
In the unlikely event that your entire family has gone out for the evening without you and that you have managed to get to a video shop and hire a film that you actually wanted to see their car will break down and they will all return with the repair man just in time to talk the entire way through the final scene.

Road maps
It is impossible to refold a road map.

Running a marathon

You should be able to run fifty miles per week on a regular basis before you try running a marathon.

Saddling a horse

Check your stirrup length from a mounted, standing position. Stirrups are properly adjusted if you can just fit the palm of your hand between your crotch and the saddle.

Sailing

No matter how strong the breeze when you leave the harbor, once you get to the furthest point from land the wind will die.

Scrabble
The one who least wants to play will win.

Seasickness
The more expensive your cabin on a cruise, the more likely it is that you will get seasick. On most luxury ships the expensive cabins are found forward, high above the waterline and with outside bulkhead exposure. This subjects them to more rolling and pitching than the less expensive cabins located nearer the waterline, inside and closer to the ship's center of gravity.

Serving drinks
When you are planning the alcohol for a party, count on two drinks per guest for the first half an hour and one drink per hour after that.

Serving wine I
Red wine should breathe for two minutes for every year between the vintage and the date of drinking.

Serving wine II
There are six glasses of wine in a bottle.

Shifting gears on a bicycle
If the gear is too high, your legs will tire before your lungs. If the gear is too low, your lungs will tire first.

Shoes
If you switch around between three pairs of shoes, they will last as long as five pairs worn out one pair at a time.

Shopping I
When shopping don't try and look for specific items, you will never find them.

Shopping II
After a hard day's shopping, the perfect item was always to be found in the very first place you looked.

Shopping malls

Shopping malls are for people who never have to go to the toilet. And never forget where they have parked their car.

Singles

On a pop album, the first and second songs on side A and the first song on side B as well as the title track will all be released as singles.

Sleep

The best two hours of sleep start exactly one hour before the alarm clock goes off.

Slinkies

Never buy more than one Slinky at a time because they will always become intertwined eventually.

Snow

Snow squeaks when the temperature is below 20 degrees.

Snow sculpture

It takes a team of three two hours to build every foot of snow sculpture.

Soap operas

If a soap opera character coughs, that character has an incurable disease and will shortly die tragically.

Swimming

Swimming a quarter of a mile is roughly equal to running one mile.

Taking photos

A professional photographer feels pleased if he or she gets one good shot for each roll of film.

Teenage driving

If you go where you're not allowed, the car will be sure to break down.

Television series

If you have ever watched one episode of a particular television series, the only time you ever catch it again it will be the same episode repeated.

Tennis

A mediocre player will sink to the level of the opposition.

Tents I
Tents with external poles are easier to pitch in high winds than tents with internal poles.

~·●·~

Tents II
Three is the optimum number for any expedition that involves carrying a tent.

~·●·~

Testing food in the wild
If you are foraging for food but are not sure about the edibility of a plant, take a small amount in your mouth, chew it, and hold it there without swallowing for five minutes. If you feel no ill effects – such as stinging, burning or numbness – swallow it and wait for eight hours. If by that time you have not experienced any cramps, pain, numbing, vomiting or diarrhea, eat another handful of the plant and wait another eight hours. If there is still no problem, consider the plant safe to eat.

Testing sunglasses

For high-altitude skiing you need very dark glasses. Look in a bathroom mirror and, if you can see your eyes, the glasses aren't dark enough.

Therapy

Therapy enables us to correct our faults by confessing our parents' shortcomings.

Throwing a pot

One pound of clay thrown with reasonable competence on a potter's wheel will make a vessel large enough to hold one average serving of most kinds of food.

Time zones
In order to avoid jet lag, change your watch to the time zone of your destination as soon as you board the plane.

Toilet paper
When traveling abroad – the softer the currency, the harder the toilet paper.

Travel
It always takes longer to get there than to get back.

Traveling by camel

Don't choose a camel that trembles while sitting. This means its front legs are weak. When traveling, take twice the money and half the clothes you think you will need.

Traveling with children

When traveling with children on holiday, at least one child will always want to go to the toilet at a point exactly equidistant between the nearest two toilets.

Tropical fish

The life expectancy of tropical fish is in direct but opposite proportion to their purchase price. A well-maintained tropical fish tank should be fully cleaned every three weeks.

Trout fishing
Trout do most of their surface feeding in the upstream third of a pool.

Tuning a stringed instrument
A stringed instrument is less apt to slip out of pitch if the strings are tuned up from flat than if it is tuned down from sharp.

Using a telescope
Stars twinkle, planets don't.

Video rental
Never rent a video from a store to which it will be inconvenient to return.

Vinyl
Long-playing records scratch and warp in direct proportion to how much their owner loves them.

Wagner
Wagner has lovely moments but awful quarters of an hour.

Walking with a backpack

At a steady pace you can walk three miles per hour without a backpack or one mile per hour with a heavy backpack.

Walking with children

The angle of incline increases in direct proportion to the number of children you are pushing.

Walking on ice

On snow-covered ice, stay away from areas without snow. This could be a sign that it is thin ice which has only recently frozen. Blue ice is safer than black ice.

Watching football
There's nothing that can happen on a football field that can't be described with a cliché.

Watching the moon
The moon rises fifty minutes later than it did the day before.

Watching waves
Every seventh wave is a big one.

Wearing jeans

On a cold day, soaking wet blue jeans will draw heat from your lower body twice as fast as wearing no jeans at all.

Weeding

When weeding, the best way to make sure that what you are pulling out is a weed is to pull on it. If it comes out of the ground easily, then it is a valuable plant.

Wine

Wine before a meal increases hunger. Wine during a meal quells the appetite. Wine at the end of a meal drowns the desire for pudding.

Winning a duel

When dueling with firearms, always aim lower than your opponent's vital organs – to pierce the heart, aim at the knees.

Yawning horses

When a horse yawns, then the weather is about to change.